Yearnings
Of a
Traveler

LEKPELE M. NYAMALON

First Published in 2016
Published by:
FORTE Publications
#12 Ashmun Street
Snapper Hill
Monrovia, Liberia

FORTE Publishing
7202 Tavenner Lane
208 Alexandria
VA, 22306

FORTE Press
76 Sarasit Road
Ban Pong, 70110
Ratchaburi, Thailand

http://fortepublishing.wix.com/fppp

Printed in the United States of America

DEDICATION

To my maternal Grandmother whom
I remember only as Yah.

.

TABLE OF CONTENTS

Acknowledgments

First to God Almighty for his grace. The most difficult part begins with thanking those behind the scenes. I'm grateful to all my English and Literature instructors throughout high school that inspired me to write. I remain in appreciation to my parents, guardians, Mulbah G. Nyamalon, Mr. Peter S.T. Marshall, Mrs. Belekula Dennis-Jeogbor for their love and support in raising a toddler to adult.

Special thanks to the Daily Observer newspaper for providing a platform for sharing my poems. I'm also grateful to the Open Society Initiative of West Africa (OSIWA) for providing an opportunity to enhance my experience through a poetry residency on Goree Island, Senegal.

Finally, to D. Othniel Forte, for his belief in me and for being so gracious to take my work from the scripts to a book. I remain sincerely grateful for the platform he has given to share my work with a greater audience.

.

Casablanca You Scared Me

When we first met
You stunned me
Fresh breeze blew your aroma my way
I admired your diversity
And saw your golden legs

But, you showed me no grace
Kept me bound in a cage, fastened, tight
Shaken! Furious! I needed an out
What was my crime? Why this animosity?

The wait was long, full of daze
Counting the hours, all in one sit
No phones, wifi-not even tea?
Casablanca, thought you were mighty.

Casablanca I'm Back

I am here again
In your wings
Did you hear that?
Don't stare at me Casablanca

Where is your hospitality?
Just a spot to sit and
Count the hours
Not a chance?

Abandoned in your arms
Dreading each moment
Counting the seconds
Casablanca...

Time

You're a healer;
You tranquilize
I heard

This is your time
Clean up the shreds
Wash up the mess

Leave behind only memories
Of you

Time
It's your turn
Take it
Imprint new memories;
Fertilize.

I Can Tell

When I stand somewhere in Gbarnga or Nimba
And see kids walking in groups
With torn out trousers, feeling dressed like stars
I can tell from their innocence that they live in their
own world
Living a dream, they wish would someday come true

When they hold hands and cross the streets
Lending a hand to each other
They inspire unity in their bonds
Clogged together like the sand
I marvel at their strength
But, I wonder, would their unity extend?
I can only wish it grows with them
I can tell from their faces that they carry the nation's
hope
Beaming with tomorrow's fate
Our Country runs around them
I can tell, they are tomorrow's people

Octopus at Ducor
(In remembrance of Operation Octopus, October 15, 1992)

Men were running amok
Smoke rising to the skies
Stirring it apart, tires blazing, children and women
marching like an ant's chariot
The walls were crashing
Here comes the Octopus!
Walking with tentacles from the breast of Mount
Barclay
Travelling beneath the rails of Bong Mines Bridge
Seeping through the pores of Bardnersville
Tearing apart the path of tomorrow's world
Where are ye mighty planners?
Hiding behind the mask of bygones be bygones?
History can't shield you boys
Thy names are carved in stone
History shall read aloud
Here comes the octopus!
Woe! Ye planners of carnage!

The face of Goree

When I saw her
She smiled broadly
But on closer look
I then saw the scars

The toil of slavery
Smell of the decay
The imprints of slaves, bundled like cattle
She couldn't speak

Smiles are elusive
I never trust them
The radiance of Goree
Hid the stories beneath

You Post Stockade

Don't smile at me
I was kept in your basement
Like a rabbit
But you never budged.

Fed like a rat
While you looked on
Beaten with cartridges
But you looked away.

Why now?
Do you need a friend?
Keep doing your thing
No one cares

I dread your name
You know it
You can't grip me
Not anymore

Inside Timbuktu

I heard you were here
The keeper of stories, buried
Deep in your attic

Timbuktu, can I have a glance?
And see the sketches of our Ancestors
How they smiled?

Maybe, from them
I might get a message
Of how to remake our land

Timbuktu, I heard you have the secrets
And stories of our warriors
Wake up Timbuktu, hold a session
Tell us what you know
Can we sit by your feet and
hear you tell those tales?

Timbuktu where are the
Clothes worn by our fathers?
Could you bring them for the world to cheer?

The path is dark-
You have the compass
Oh Timbuktu, our hope, lead us

Timbuktu; could you testify?
Set the stage for a new Africa?
Oh Timbuktu! We need you.

You're A Precious Jewel
Poem to a little girl

Jewel, my dear jewel
You're pretty, witty; a jewel
You're a beauty, bright and precious
You are a meal, tasty and delicious
When it's hot, your kiss is cold
And milky as ice-cream
Cooling the warmth, hot and making a day's dream

Your face glitters like the morning Sun
Lighting up the day with beams, cheers and fun
Reaping through the pores of a man's world with love
And smashing his heartbeat like a clean white dove

Jewel my dear jewel if you get me just a little space
in your heart
I'll be glad; I'd find a warm shelter, smiling on a chariots
cart
Oh precious, slender, dark and blonde with a pretty
little voice, quiet but bold
My precious Jewel, your memories shall forever be told

I Will Never Sell You Again My Brother

My brother, hold my hands as I vow
Before the moon, the sun and earth
With sweat pouring from my brow
Mixed with my tears of anguish, fear
Hear me out, please!
I will never sell you again

You and I could build the walls and farms
Our hands can break a mountain
We can dig and make a road
Beneath the Nile
We can clear the fields and grow
Our plantation to feed the world

My brother, this is a pledge
Hold my wrist, let's make a covenant
Upon our ancestors' blood,
We will rebuild our land
And make it flow like a fountain

You see, you plow over there;
Grew rice, corn and wheat
Yet, our children die of hunger
While others are malnourished
But we worked our lives building your mines
Industry, railroads and bridges

Now, with empty hands
We gaze at Africa
No, not again!
I'll not fall for the tricks
I'll not sell you to strangers
Nor will I sell you to those
With briefcases of money-
For our oil, gold and diamonds

They come with magic,
To tear us apart
They fund civil wars
To destroy our heritage
Bring your hands, brother.
Let's fight together
Let us make our ancestors
Smile from their graves

No! I will never sell you again.

Dig The Graves

Where are we now Africa?
Often I ask.
The truck is stuck. Where are the men?
Sometimes, I want to grasp the diggers
And burst the graves
Plead to the bones of our fathers
Come back! Come back, please!

Standing on the grave of Lumumba
I heard him sobbing for a continent
With eyes as red as mercury,
Wishing he could rise again

Where is our courage?
Is it lost in greed; stuck in fame?
Has it taken on wings and soared away?

Bring home Sankara and Cabral
Tell Nkrumah and Toure' the table is set
Oh Nyerere your seat is kept
The banquet is on, you are needed
Dig the graves and bring out Senghor
Ay Madiba your strength is needed
Dig the graves and gather the sons of our land
Your bravery must save our continent heroes,
Please live again or breathe through your sons
We need you here, more than the graves.

Holding Our Fathers' Bags

To ye sons of today
Hold you tightly those bags of time
With fist knitted, clutched to the handle
And cuddle them under your arms

Keep from the smell of termites and maggots
Lest they chew and swallow from history's plate
As you walk miles across the Atlantic
Roaming through forests, darker than dusk

Hold on firmly the bags of time
Ever wonder why?
In those bags are tales of warriors-
And their conquest lands and clans
Beating down tribes and marching on ropes

Sealed are paintings of beautiful lakes
Hovered by mangrove swamps
And crocodiles swimming like ships sailing on the
Mediterranean
And birds soaring in space like rockets

Stuck are carvings of ages -a life story retold
Of kings riding on chariots and camels, flying across
the Sahara
With vibrations of songs of princes and rhythms
flowing from the mouth of pigeons
And humming of the guinea fowls, with speeches
echoed by parrots

Dare not drop those bags child, or lose your footing
As a ship lost from the compass, or a flight swayed
from the radar
You'll stare like a stranger from
afar with history forgotten
And time will spit you away; you'll be wrapped and
trashed in the ocean

Open that bag, unveil the treasure and spill the gifts
of olden
We'll sit around the fire hearths and pin the puzzles
of Bushrod Island
To the shores of lake Retba and glue the basin of
Kintampo waterfalls
To the dew-capped mountains of mount Cameroon,
we'll paint the peak of Kilimanjaro

And sketch the back of Cape Verde and mend the
pieces of the Gambia
To the great rift valley, and the green farmland of
Harare
And craft the coastal lands of the Atlantic; we'll
uncover the treasures of Timbuktu
And view the cultural village of Lesedi.

We'll dig the bones of Askia the Great and place
them in a golden showcase
We'll oil the sword of Mansa Musa and stand it in a
marble stone

We'll weave the images of Sundiata Keita
                    We'll shout to the world that the
                    Hippopotamus is Africa's pet

We'll tour the Sapo Park and count our species
That'll be a day when our memory returns
We will tell our history. Tell of our fathers
Everyone hush...its story time.

I Am The Black Root

Like the crust at the base of a cooked hot rice
I hold the bottom and keep it warm
With bent back, holding the heat, until a decent
cooked meal is served
When done, I'm thrown to the pit, not served in
regular dishes

I am the bone that coats the marrow
I offer my frame for flesh to grow
Till it's fat and ready, grilled and served in style
Then, I, the bone, am thrown to the dogs

I am the dumb truck that ignited the engines of
industries
Like robots, we lit up the skies
Like bulldozers, cleared the plantations of the world
And plowed the fields like oxen
Producing plenty of wheat, corn and grain
And when the light was set at twilight
I was shipped in tankers bundled back to the dustbin
before dawn

And where did civilization breed?
On the backdoors of Kansas, or somewhere in the
arctic?

Or did it light on the shores of the Nile- the door steps of Africa?

You may write it twisted or flawed
But the mind pushes the pen
And Africa-my birthplace knows its story
I am a dark, black and bold man
Born and bred from the root of Africa
And I'm proud!

My Body Is Gold
{Poem to end violence against women}

Ever tried to break gold?
With your bare hand?
Did you feel the stiff?
Would you trade gold for brass?
Or try to sweep it like some grass?
Gold is a precious shiny stone-not a straw
My body –this body you see, is gold

I may be short, small or huge
With my lappa stained with red palm oil
Swamped by crying babies in the kitchen
Or, I may be carrying my bucket,
Filled with pepper, okra, and corn
But with these, I put food on that table
Can't you see my courage shines like a lightening?

I may be walking in mud down waterside
But I smile like the bright morning sun
Does that make me a cow that you beat to move?

Why do you knock me down and gang rape me
Like hungry thirsty leopards?
And you laugh like it's funny?
Am I sweeter than honey?
You are a coward, cruel and shameless

Why do you keep me dirty, barefooted and broken?
Are you afraid of the radiance in my eyes?
Do you fear the glamour of my beauty?
Are you struck by the size of my hips?
Are you intimidated by the glow of my breasts?

Now, hear me young man
This body you beat is gold
Are you a beast, built to beat a woman?
If you're Hercules, why not jump on a lion in his den?
Is your prowess fixed for women?

But, you don't know gold
Someday, you'll see a real man
A man with arms thicker than yours
And chest wide for my body
With voice that vibrates like thunder
And hands stronger than oxen
But, he, like a knight, guards me like a queen
And guess what?
This man, my man, is a real man
Like a miner, he knows gold, even in dirt
And he cleans it up and sets it in a jar
And marvels at the splendor-enjoying his treasure
But, you poor man
You were blinded by a ghost
Never knew the gold you had
And boy, oh boy, when you know this

I'll flee like a bird and be gone
When it hits your door, you'd be done
Left with your over grown ego
Chained in a cage
Stuck with your rage

Did you think you could dim my bulb?
And blow my lamp
I'll still be on fire
When we pass you by
Rolling your wheelbarrow on the outskirts of Duala
You'll hide your face behind the mountain's back
With your torn-out trousers, asking in your colloqua
da my woman there?

This face you bruise is gold
This nose you punch is gold
This arm you twist is gold
This leg you sweep is gold
This body, my body is gold.

My Sister Beretta

My sister Beretta
Who are you?
You spit venom like a loose cobra
Splashing across your preys

How could you be my sister
When you split the head of my father?
Or shattered his brain as an egg?
You might be a vampire

Are you my sister that shook our village?
Our own small town?
Sending our brothers on heels?
Turning over our clan like an earthquake?
With dust dancing in the skies?

Oh sister Beretta...ay yah
You are cursed oh sister
Your face is buried in black
With pimples wide like pot-holes

Your hands pierce like thorns
Piercing the hands of your carriers
Slave to your menace
Cowed by your threats
Sister Beretta you're ruthless

Cold blooded and mad
You chest is bare, stolen heart
You're a beast, not my sister!

The Hut Taxpayer

I was chased
Knocked down
Bundled and beaten
To pay my share

What was my crime?
To live and breathe
In the same space
I had to pay a price.

What was my fare?
Anything I owned
My goats, chickens, mats or cutlass
I was held a captive
I was the intruder
Trespassing on a field
Reserved-
Yet I kept it clean-not for me

I was the hut taxpayer
My grandfather was
My uncle was
And we lived in huts
Built with our hands
While our taxes soared
We sat and watched
Our beneficiaries glowed in style
Living in castles built from our hut taxes.

The Stench Of Slavery

They came with a mind
To destroy the birth and soul of a people
They strapped in chains the hope of a world
And whisked to build their own

They took the seeds and grew in their barns
And broke the spirit of a continent
Shattering the dream and masking the beauty
They tore to shreds the history
And stole the golden culture
Burned the artifacts and blocked her memory

Why slavery? Why Africa?
What did you see?
On your conscience lives the guilt of her blood
Sacrifices on your plantations, to start the engines of
your industry

And lit your skies with scrapers
Why slavery?
I can feel you claws reaching for my arms
Sniffing for my hearts to rip open

And spill my blood
I can hear your roar as I run for cover
I can feel your legs in the dark searching for my
limbs

I dread your stench
You're a coward, a beast
But, Africa is coming back with a might bigger than yours
And you'll bury your face in the sand
This time, you'll be a slave to your stench.

Scars Of A Tired Nation

What more can a country take?
Stories of children that can't live in peace
Treating each other like strangers from afar
The sons returning and the ones they met
Fighting for a space left by Mama

1980-panic splashed upon the face of Africa's oldest
child
Bringing down the walls a century high
Building another 100 ft higher
Shaking to shreds young old mama
Promising her a lie to leave her alone

What a tired country she has become
Standing alone on a continent she blossomed
Left alone by countries she led to Independence
A troubled house is always lonely
Such a land she stands to be
Her place in history forgotten by men of time
Left to maggots and bugs to chew
And spit into history's shredder
Her prints erased from the archives of Africa's
glossary
And left to wander- gathering crumbs

Couldn't her sons keep her diary?
Of how generous a home she had
Giving a shelter for Africa's neglected
Spewing hope into a lifeless continent

Doomed by colonialism and whisked by fear

She went in shock and comatose
For 14 years her eyes couldn't blink nor wink
Only ears of thunder and terror
With a sigh of relief to live again
Her candle is lit in a thunderstorm

The scars of a tired nation are eating up again
The face of EBOLA shatters the dream
To put together a wretched lonely life
Could this scar flip into a star?
And shine forever?

Thought You Were My Brother

When the day snubbed you
And the night could hide you not
In my arms you ran
And we cried together

Our tears bathed us like rainfall
As we stuck like glue-sobbing
When the bulldozer smashed your matchbox houses
In my zinc shacks we cuddled
Over a lump of sugar and gari

When your Country called you a stranger
You became a member of my household
We sat and planned
Fanning ourselves with the nighttime heat
I gave you money from my susu club
And took you underground for years
Your heroes were my heroes
We were a family

When we grew, we pushed down our monster
We broke it to the ground like a cotton tree
And we cheered, our nightmare was over

Then, I became a stranger
You stare at me like cockroaches
And chase me like rabbits
Whip me with shambars
And bruise me with machetes

Tearing my clothes to shreds

Why?
What is my crime?
Thought we were blood?

TShabalala, Masekela,
Makeba, Courtney, Mbali,
Nthabiseng, Nokuthula,
OLWETHU, Thandeka...
I hear a deafening silence

Thought I had a brother in SOWETO

Ode To My Jailer

Cheer up! Son of a monster
I love you though-
Your specialty is torture
Schooled to beat and bruise
You made me a gladiator

I feel the pains curving on my back
From the whips of your cartridge
You made me a warrior
I hear the barking of your voice
Roaring like a strangled lion
Hungry for my blood
You jeered at my tears
They made me a soldier
You tried to dump my soul
But, you shot my ego in the sky
I can walk on broken glass
Cuz my heart is stiff like the back of steel
I'm no more a crying prisoner
Mocked by his captor
Driven to death
I'm now a storyteller
Molded by you
My jailer, thank you!
Your boots made my eyes sharper than eagles'
My wings wider than falcons
My courage fiercer than a furnace
I'm a fighter
The medal is yours!

My Brother Drowned Crossing

The hopes soared
Of a trip to wonderland
And behold the majesties
Live it in awe

On Scary paths
Through thorns and stones
With bruises greeting his feet
A daring journey began

From Banjui to Dakar
To Bamako and Tripoli
The trip seemed awesome
Then gloomy and fearful

They were parked like luggage
Stuffed in the depth of that boat
Air was priceless
The flight was nigh

Then, the rain began
Every man his life to keep
The swimming contest ensue

Dive or drown for the medal

The participants were curious
Khalifa, Gassama, Abdul, Denja
Bakari, Kofi, Abeji, Abikanile

Aba, Abayomi, Ayodele, Asabi, Marjani, Olabisi

My brothers, where are you going?
On to rekindle dreams of diamond paved streets?
And brush the gold-plated walls with your sweat?
Look at your farm Africa

Just look beneath the soil
And see gold, diamonds, iron, oil
Why are you crossing?

Beneath the ocean where you dived
Did you see the fish, aquariums?
And starfish cross over?
Live your dream my brother
Make your space your dream land

Sackie, Vambah, Enoch, Kwame, Quincy
Dorley, Losene, Nimely
I heard you in a meeting
To join the Olympics
See your brothers gasping in the Mediterranean
My brothers-
And you Mr. Hon
You drive an SUV a hundred thousand
With no buses to ferry students
And my brothers dived like fish

Osman, Abu, Khalifa, Ayodele, those bodies are not
Olympic loosers
Not poisoned fish
They are warm blooded mammals

Frozen like ice
My brother is one of them
My brother drowned crossing

Citizen ID Card

I was told to get an identity
Wrapped in a plastic sheet
With my name and County
I was smiling when looking at the cameras
And watched the lights beam and
Flash!
I had an ID card
A proud citizen of my Country
I remember the moment

Then the year came
It was 1990
My identity was a poison
I was hunted like chickens
By gangs hungry for my blood
I ran in swamps and slept with frogs
My ID card was a nightmare
I was chased like flies pursuing a corpse

Why?
Why did I smile at that camera that took my face?
I was putting my face on death roll for a mobster
Citizen ID card...
I will never smile at you again

Belle Yalla

...you know the stories
I can repeat one by one
Now you're lonely
Captured by thorns and shrubs
Where are your buddies?
Can you take the stand?
Belle Yalla...
Take this moment and free your soul
You heard the screams
The echoing sounds of rattans
The kicks of boots
The fainting noise of gunshots
You saw the bruises
The airtaxis come and go
You were a cheerleader
Then, your name soared in space
Many awe at your feigned prominence
Your imagined majesty
Standing on legs of bronze
Living on a ranch
But you kept a lion's den
You were a scavenger
Your memory has stories to tell
Why not write a book?
Belle Yalla..
You can't survive this
Let's strike a deal
Get your immunity
Take the stand...

Forgotten Future

We don't crave the stars
But a light to shine on our paths
That we stumble not

Not the moon
Just a space to play at night
And beam with innocence

We hope not for diamonds
But a precious gift of dignity
Buried beneath our ground

Let our girls live
And go to school too
Spare them from rape and genital mutilation

Our little boys aren't men
For arms and drugs
Leave them

Give the earth when you're done
We might need it
Free from pollution

We need a life
At least once
Is that hard?

Here We Are

We are the sons of travelers
Of men who walked miles in search of home
They slept in deserts
And sailed on oceans
Roaming the forests for a land they could own
Now,
When the plantations needed us no more
Like garbage our site was set
We were thrown to rot
But never did
Others came back
Rescued from the fangs
That chained us
Now, we're stuck
The brotherhood of freedom
The off springs of the Mayflower
The Kpelleh, the Kru, the Mano, the Gio, the Lorma,
the Dan, the Mende, the Kwa, the Negros' den
They folded us from all sides
To chew our space
From Mount Nimba, Bo, Cavalla,
When we said we were free
They looked another way
Like orphans, our cries were ours
This is the theatre of the black man's hall
Enmeshed by the hollowness

We're a painting of hopes
Of desert travelers, Traders,
Farmers, blacksmiths, runaway slaves,
The Graincoast hustlers
Our identity is wrapped in a cloth
Of one million colors
The tye-dye nation
Of the illiterate, the literate
The peasants, the diasporas, the locals
The neck-tie roamers, the rolled up sleeves
The cowl bowl sellers, the pehn-pehn riders
We went to bed with anarchy and got
Up a smiling people
Risen from hell
The Sun is set for a new day
And,
Here we are

About The Author

Lekpele M. Nyamalon from Liberia is an OSIWA Poetry fellow, an up and coming writer, poet, essayist and collector of traditional short stories. His Poem 'Forgotten Future' was selected as the winning poem for World Poetry Day competition in 2015 organized by 'Young People Today'- a youth-based sexuality and reproductive health initiative in South Africa. Lekpele has an arts and culture startup dubbed the 'Moonlight Theatre' and has embarked on a village writing project called the 'Moonlight Series.' His Poems have been featured in several publications including the Kalahari Review and an upcoming OSIWA Anthology of West African Poems. He is also the founder of Africa's life, a non-for profit initiative to inspire youths through motivational speaking. Lekpele holds an MBA in Finance from Cuttington University in Liberia. here

COMING SOON!!!!!

MY FULL LENGTH POETRY BOOK.
WATCH OUT!!!

www.ingramcontent.com/pod-product-compliance
Lightning Source LLC
Chambersburg PA
CBHW060056050426
42448CB00011B/2479